CUTTING HOLES e.g. e

1 Lay a thick wad of newspaper
   a craft knife or scissors acros
   to cut out

2 Starting from this slit, careful
   your shape

3 Piece by piece, carefully cut round the piece you want to cut out

INTRODUCTION

All the items in this book are inexpensive to make and many use materials found around the home.

You may need a little help from an adult to make some of the things but you will be proud to give any of the presents to your family or friends.

Some of the ideas will help to make a special occasion even more special.

You will need a pencil and a pair of scissors as well as the other materials listed and always remember to lay newspaper over your work surface before you start.

how to make
Presents

by LAURA GUNSTENSEN DTD
and JEAN TEMPLE DA

photographs by
TIM CLARK

Ladybird Books Ltd
Loughborough 1978

PAPER FLOWERS

You will need:

3 packets of good quality crêpe paper (different colours)
green crêpe paper
thin green garden canes
'Sellotape'
green PVC tape

Leave the crêpe paper folded as you bought it and cut three wads (one from each colour) 4″ (10·2cm), 5″ (12·7cm) and 7″ (17·8cm) deep. Cut out the shapes as shown by the dotted lines on the diagrams.

Starting with the shape in Fig 1, 'Sellotape' the bottom edge of the crêpe paper to the top of the garden cane. Unfold the crêpe paper and wind it round the cane, 'Sellotaping' it at intervals to keep it in place. Wind a final layer of 'Sellotape' around the base of the crêpe paper to fix it securely to the cane.

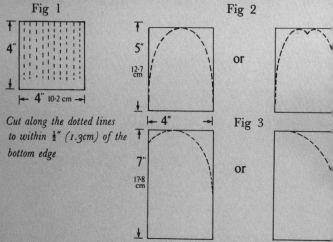

Fig 1

4″

|← 4″ 10·2 cm →|

Cut along the dotted lines to within ½″ (1.3cm) of the bottom edge

Fig 2

5″

12·7 cm

|← 4″ →|

or

Fig 3

7″

17·8 cm

|← 4″ →|

or

When you have finished with the first section of the crêpe paper do the same with the second and third colours (Figs 2 and 3), pinching and gathering each petal shape at the base as you wind it on. Take care to 'Sellotape' the crêpe paper firmly to the cane.

When the three sections are complete, finish it by wrapping some leaf shapes cut from the green crêpe paper around the stem to cover the base of the flower. Use the green PVC tape to secure these.

Gently pull out each petal and stretch the crêpe to make the petals fuller and rounded at the top.

VALENTINE CARD

Fold the two pieces of coloured paper in half and draw a $4\frac{1}{2}''$ (11·4cm) square on each, using the folded edge as one side of the square. On both pieces, on the sides opposite the fold, draw semi-circles then cut away the shaded area shown on the diagram (Fig 1).

Divide the squares into strips, and cut from the folded edge inwards for about $4\frac{3}{4}''$ (12cm). If you open out your folded pieces, they should both look like Fig 1.

Now fold them again and weave the strips from one piece of paper through the strips of the other as shown in Fig 2. When this has been done they should form a heart-shaped pocket (Fig 3).

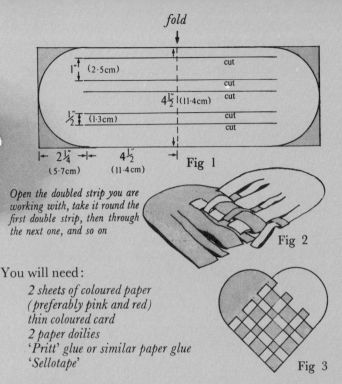

fold

1" (2·5cm)

cut

cut

4½" (11·4cm)

cut

½" (1·3cm)

cut

cut

2¼ (5·7cm)   4½ (11·4cm)

Fig 1

Open the doubled strip you are working with, take it round the first double strip, then through the next one, and so on

Fig 2

You will need:

> 2 sheets of coloured paper
> (preferably pink and red)
> thin coloured card
> 2 paper doilies
> 'Pritt' glue or similar paper glue
> 'Sellotape'

Fig 3

Use the finished heart as a template to cut two more hearts from the coloured card. Trim them down slightly so that when they are 'Sellotaped' together along their straight edges, they will fit inside the first heart as a lining.

Cut the edges from two paper doilies to fit the curved edges of the second heart. Glue these edges to the card so that when the lining is in place, the doilies can be seen.

Write the greeting on the outside of the card, and put a small present such as a handkerchief or sweets inside the pocket.

POMPOMS AND A POMPOM ANIMAL

You will need:
balls of different coloured wool
thick card
an egg box
2 beads
poster paints
glue

There are two ways of making pompoms. The first is to take a piece of thick card about 3″ (7·6cm) square and wind the wool around it as shown in Fig 1 until you have a thick layer of wool. Carefully remove the card and tie the bundle of wool tightly around the middle using some more of the wool (Fig 2). Cut through the loops of wool, fluff out the pompom and trim it to shape. This kind of pompom is best made using thick wool.

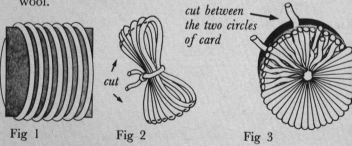

cut

cut between the two circles of card

Fig 1   Fig 2   Fig 3

The other way is to cut two circles from thick card, each about 3″ (7·6cm) across. Cut a 1″ (2·5cm) hole in the centre of each, and place the cards together. Wind the wool over and over the rings until the hole in the middle has been filled up.

Snip through the wool at the edges of the rings, and gently pull the rings apart. Tie some wool tightly round the wool between the rings (Fig 3) and then pull the rings off. Fluff out the pompom and trim it to shape.

To make the hedgehog shown in the picture, make a pompom using the first method. Then cut a piece from the centre of the base of an egg box to make the nose. Paint the nose, using poster paints, and sew on two beads for eyes. Glue it in position by pushing a section of the pompom into the nose. Trim the pompom to make the shape of the animal.

Other animals can be made by gluing bits of felt for eyes, feet, ears or tails. Several pompoms can be sewn together to make a snake.

FELT JEWELLERY

You will need:

    scraps of felt
    fancy buttons
    beads and sequins
    petersham ribbon
    'Velcro'
    safety pins
    glue (e.g. 'Bostik')
    'Vilene' stiffening

NOTE: When cutting symmetrical shapes like those opposite, draw half the shape on a folded piece of paper. Cut it out while still folded and then open out

BRACELET

Cut a length of ribbon to fit your wrist comfortably with 1½" (4cm) extra. Hem the ends and stitch a small piece of 'Velcro' on each end. Stitch flowers (Fig 1) to the centre of the length of ribbon and decorate it with sequins, buttons and beads.

NECKLACE

This is made in the same way as the bracelet. Cut a small fringe in felt and stitch it to the centre before fixing the flowers in place.

BROOCH

Draw the butterfly shape (Fig 2) as large as you want it and make a paper pattern. Using this, cut out the butterfly in felt and stiffening. Glue the stiffening to the back of the felt. Decorate it with small pieces of felt, sequins and buttons, glued or stitched into place. Stitch a safety pin onto the back.

HAIR ORNAMENT

Cut three or four flower shapes (Fig 1) and stitch a bead to the centre of each. Stitch them to a felt fringe which is folded double. Sew this onto an elastic ring.

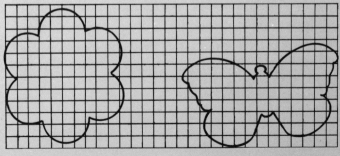

Fig 1   Fig 2

WINDMILL

You will need:

thin coloured card or acetate film
a piece of stiff wire about 6" (15cm) long
2 beads
a thin bamboo cane

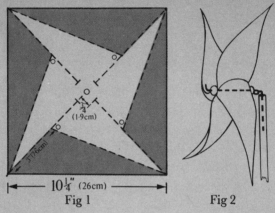

Fig 1   Fig 2

Draw the shape shown in Fig 1 onto the coloured card (or acetate film) and cut it out along the dotted lines. Make five holes as shown.

Decorate the windmill by using coloured paper, paint or shapes cut from coloured gummed paper.

Take the piece of wire and bend it as shown in Fig 2. Thread one of the beads onto the wire and then push the wire through the centre hole of the windmill from the back. Take each corner of the windmill in turn and carefully bend it over towards the centre passing the wire through the holes.

Fit the other bead onto the wire and bend the wire over to stop the bead from coming off (the distance between the beads should be about 2″ (5cm)). Push the other end of the wire down the hollow stem of the bamboo cane.

DOOR SIGN

You will need :
coloured cardboard
brass paper fastener
poster paint
glue
squared paper with 1" (2·5cm) squares

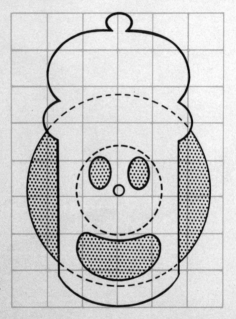

Copy the diagram of the face onto the squared paper, making it as large as you want it, and cut it out. Lay the paper pattern onto the coloured card, and cut out the card. Cut out holes for eyes and a mouth. (See how to do this at the front of the book.)

Cut out two circles in card of different colours. One should be a little larger than the width of the face and a smaller one, 1½″ (4cm) less across the middle. Pierce the centre of each circle and glue the smaller onto the larger, matching up the centres.

Paint the face carefully as in the picture. Pierce the face at the centre dot and fasten the circles in place with the brass fastener. Write messages in the mouth and draw in the eyes to make different expressions. The larger circle shows the mouth and the smaller circle shows the eyes.

WIND CHIMES

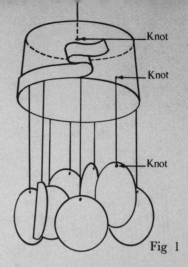

You will need:

3 cartons of various sizes and shapes

button thread and needle

milk bottle tops

coloured paper, material or poster paints

Fig 1

To make the wind chimes shown in the picture a 'Smartie' tube, yogurt carton and margarine tub were used. If the container you are using has a double rim, cut away the outer rim using scissors.

Paint the cartons or cover them with coloured paper or material. Round out the milk bottle tops. Suspend them from the rims of the containers with button thread so that they hang down for about 4" (10cm). Stick a strip of material or paper round the rim of the carton to cover the knots (see Fig 1).

Thread the three sections of the wind chimes together, knotting the thread to keep each carton in place. Sew a loop of ribbon onto the top of the upper carton.

If you suspend the wind chimes in a doorway or window, where there is a draught, the bottle tops will hit each other and make a tinkling sound.

17

GONK

You will need:

a cardboard cup	*the base cut from a yogurt carton*
a small plastic tub	*a drawing pin*
a cardboard egg box	*silver paper (cooking foil)*
a polystyrene egg box	*glue (e.g. 'Bostik')*
lollipop stick	*poster paint*
wool	

Turn your cardboard cup upside down. The spectacles and nose are cut from the fastening flap of a polystyrene egg box. Paint them and glue them into position on the cup. Cut two arms from a cardboard egg box. Paint them and leave them to dry.

Paint a lollipop stick and when it is dry, push it into a slit cut into one of the arms. Glue the arms into position.

To make the hair, wind wool around a piece of cardboard approximately 8″ (20cm) long and cut the hank of wool at both ends. Tie the pieces together in the middle. Glue the hair onto the top of the cup.

Make the hat from a plastic tub covered with silver paper. Glue it into place.

The moustache is made in the same way as the hair, but using a smaller piece of cardboard about 4″ (10cm) long.

Make the shield from the base of a yogurt carton covered in silver paper. Push a drawing pin through the middle and glue it into place on the other arm.

COVERED BOX

You will need:

    small box
    pieces of material
    broderie anglaise (optional)
    cotton wool
    elastic
    glue (e.g. 'Bostik')
    thick card

Cut a piece of material big enough to cover the base and sides of the box. Cut away a small square from each corner to reduce the folded thickness. Stand the box in the centre, fold the material neatly up the sides, then glue it to the inside of the box.

The box is lined with a 'bag' of material with elasticated edges folded over the rim to grip the sides. To make this, cut a square of material for the base of the box, allowing for seams. Cut a strip of material to line the four sides. (Allow extra length for gathering and extra width for the seam and the fold over the rim.) Make a seam for the elastic along one edge, gather the other edge, and sew it to the base. Place the lining inside the box, stretching the elastic over the rim.

To make the lid, cut a square of card large enough to sit on top of the box. Place this on the material and cut out a square 1½″ (4cm) bigger than the card. Now spread a layer of cotton wool over one side of the card. This will be the top side of the lid. Cover this with the material and carefully fold the edges over and glue them to the other side of the card. Cut a second square of material the same size as your lid. Neatly hem the raw edges and then either stitch or glue this square to the underside of the lid.

If you like, you can decorate your box with broderie anglaise.

MASKS

You will need:

coloured card
silver card or silver paint
crêpe paper

glue (e.g. 'Bostik')
brass paper fasteners

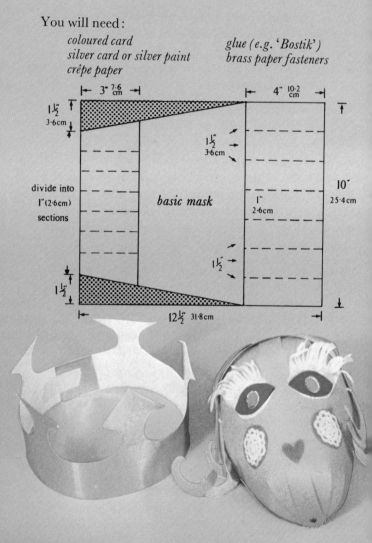

divide into 1" (2·6cm) sections

basic mask

3" 7·6 cm

4" 10·2 cm

1½" 3·6cm

1½" 3·6cm

1" 2·6cm

1" 2·6cm

10" 25·4 cm

1½"

1½"

12½" 31·8cm

The basic mask is made from card measuring $12\frac{1}{2}'' \times 10''$ (31·8cm × 25·4cm), divided up as shown in the diagram. Cut away the shaded area and cut along the dotted lines to form slits along the two short edges. Join the strips together by bringing the two outer strips in to overlap slightly, followed by each pair in turn.

When all the strips are gathered together, pierce through the overlapping area and fix all the pieces together with a brass paper fastener. The other end is made in the same way.

Stick your decorations onto the basic mask. You can make a crown or helmet to wear with your masks. Cut out of card and fasten with tape, to fit your head.

BASKET OF SWEETS

You will need:

> 2 margarine cartons
> crêpe paper in two colours
> coloured tissue paper
> home made fudge
> silver paper (cooking foil)
> gift tie ribbon
> glue (e.g. 'Bostik')
> brass paper clips

Cut a circle of crêpe paper 12″ (30cm) across and cover the outside of one margarine carton, folding the edges over, onto the inside of the carton. Glue this into place on the inside edge of the carton.

Cut a strip of plastic $\frac{1}{2}$″ × $9\frac{1}{2}$″ (1cm × 24cm) from the side of the other margarine carton to form the handle. Bind it with crêpe paper $1\frac{1}{2}$″ × 20″ (4cm × 50cm), and fix the handle into place with the two brass paper clips.

Cut a rectangle of crêpe paper 3″ × 12″ (7·5cm × 30cm) in a different colour. This makes the lining of the basket.

Cut a circle of crêpe paper $4\frac{1}{2}$″ (11·5cm) across in the same colour as the rectangle. Cut off the base of the second carton and cover this with the circle of crêpe paper. Glue the edges down to the back of the plastic. Place the covered circle of plastic, wrong side down, firmly in the bottom of the basket so that it holds the lining in place.

Make the paper flowers by placing together two tissue paper circles 2″ (5cm) across. Pinch the double tissue together in the centre and glue it to the handle.

Wrap the sweets in silver foil and small ribbons. Tie a ribbon round the basket, finishing with a big bow.

Fig 1

Fig 2

ADVENT CALENDAR

You will need:

garden cane
Christmas wrapping thread
coloured paper or foil
old Christmas cards
glue (e.g. 'Bostik')

Cut out 24 circles $2\frac{1}{2}''$ (6·4cm) across from coloured paper or foil. Cut out one star shape as shown in Fig 1.

Cut out 25 round pictures from old Christmas cards, making them about $1\frac{1}{2}''$ (3·8cm) across. Glue the pictures onto the centres of the coloured circles and the star, sandwiching the end of a length of the wrapping thread between each two circles (Fig 2). This thread will be used to hang the pictures.

Fringe each circle by cutting in towards the centre as shown in the diagram. On the back of each circle paint or stick large numbers from 1 to 24. On the back of the star stick number 25. The numbers can be cut from an old calendar. Arrange the circles in four rows with the star at the bottom and hang them from the garden cane with the thread.

Hang the garden cane on a wall using the wrapping thread with the numbers facing outwards. On the first of December turn the card numbered 1 to show the picture, then turn a card each day, until at last the star is turned on Christmas Day.

DESK TIDY

You will need:
>5 plastic washing-up liquid bottles
>coloured wrapping paper
>stiff cardboard
>pieces of felt
>white PVC tape
>glue

Cut the plastic bottles to various heights, the ones in the picture are 5″, 4″, 3″, 2″ and 1″ (12·7, 10·2, 7·6, 5·1 and 2·5cm) respectively. Wrap coloured paper around each bottle and glue it in position. Strengthen the top edges by binding them with white PVC tape.

Group the bottles together as shown in the picture and place them on top of the stiff cardboard. Draw round the outside of the group on the card and cut this shape out. Glue the bottles to the base and apply dabs of glue where the sides touch each other.

Cover the underside of the base with felt, and glue circles of felt on the inside base of the two smallest pots.

Use the desk tidy to keep pens, rulers, brushes, paper clips, pins and rubbers tidy.

Decide on the items you are putting in your desk tidy before cutting the bottle to the appropriate height

cut here

cut here

RECORDER CASE

You will need:
   1 yard ½" braid (90cm × 1cm)
   2 yards 1½" wide cotton webbing (1·8m × 4cm)
   (instead of cotton webbing, you can use felt 3" × 36"
   8cm × 90cm)
   thread
   elastic
   2 buttons

Cut the cotton webbing in half and stitch the two long edges together to form a strip 36" (90cm) long by 3" (8cm) wide. Stitch the woven braid over this join to hide it. Make a double hem at each end and then fold the strip to form a bag about 16" (41cm) long leaving about 3" (6cm) for the flap. Stitch the outer edges together with blanket stitch. Sew on buttons and make button loops on the flap with elastic.

The felt bag is made in the same way, but does not need braid. Decorate the bag with felt flowers or shapes before stitching the sides together.

You can make bags for pencils or knitting needles in the same way.

CHRISTMAS
MOBILE

You will need:

    thin coloured card
    coloured foil in different colours
    gold poster paint
    flesh coloured gummed paper
    Christmas gift wrapping thread
    or black button thread
    stiff wire
    glue (e.g. 'Bostik')

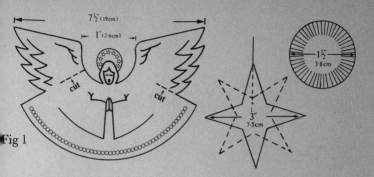

Fig 1

The stars are cut from the coloured foil using the pattern shown in the diagram (make them about 3" [7·5cm] across). Glue two of these star shapes together to make an eight-pointed star, and place the end of a length of thread between them. This thread is used to hang the stars. Decorate some of the stars by cutting circles of foil 1½" (3·8cm) across and fringing the edges by cutting towards the centre in thin strips. Glue a circle to the centre of each star.

The angel is cut from coloured card (see Fig 1). Decorate her, using gold poster paint. Glue flesh-coloured gummed paper over the hands and face, and draw on the face.

When the angel has been cut out, decorate the back of the wings, using the gold paint. Cut along the dotted lines and slot the wings together. Glue a length of thread to the back of the angel and hang her from the centre of a length of stiff wire about 12" (30cm) long. Suspend the stars from the ends of smaller lengths of wire and assemble the mobile as shown in the picture. Each wire can be balanced by moving the thread from which it hangs, along the wire.

BIRTHDAY OR MOTHER'S DAY CARD

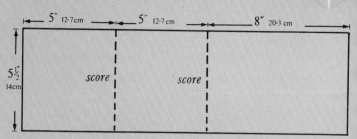

You will need:
> *coloured tissue paper*
> *white card*
> *gummed coloured paper*
> *or poster paints*
> *felt-tip pens*
> *'Pritt' glue or similar paper glue*

5" 12·7cm	5" 12·7cm	8" 20·3 cm
	score	*score*

5½" 14cm

Cut a piece of white card 5½" (14cm) by 18" (45·7cm) and score along the dotted lines as shown in the diagram. Fold the card into a zigzag shape.

Open the card out and use either green paint or coloured paper to make the grass. Try to do this so that when the card is folded up there is a continuous band of green.

Make the flowers by cutting several flower shapes from folded tissue paper of different colours and sizes. Open out the shapes and stick them to the card by gluing them at the centres only. Use several layers of flower shapes to make up each flower. Decorate the flower centres by using coloured paper or felt-tip pens.

Cut the stems and leaves of the flowers from green gummed paper and stick them into position. Draw the butterfly, using felt-tip pens.

Write the greeting on the card using your best handwriting or 'Letraset'.

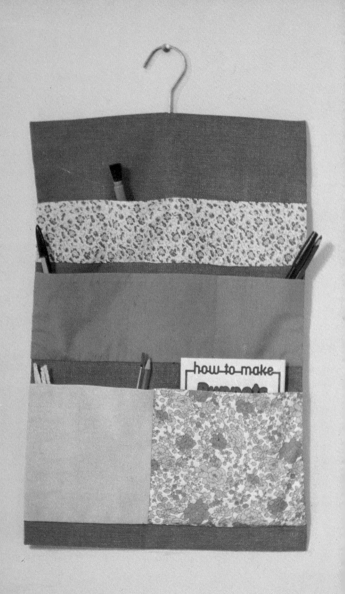

WALL POCKETS

You will need:
> *a piece of material* 24″ × 15″ *(60cm × 37·5cm)*
> *4 pieces of contrasting material for pockets*
>> 14″ × 3½″ *(35cm × 9cm)*
>> 14″ × 5″ *(35cm × 13cm)*
>> 6½″ × 7″ *(16·5cm × 18cm)*
>> 8″ × 7″ *(20cm × 18cm)*
>
> *a child's wooden coathanger*

Fold over 3″ (7·5cm) at the top of the main piece of material right sides together. Stitch down each side edge with a ¾″ (2cm) seam. Turn this flap right side out and iron it. It should be at the top on the back of the main piece of material. Sew a ¾″ (2cm) double hem round the other two sides and the bottom of the material.

Cut out the material for the pockets. Think carefully about colours and patterns. Hem the top edge of each pocket. Press under, with an iron, ½″ (1cm) on the other three edges, and then carefully pin into place, starting with the two base pockets. Stitch the three edges by hand or machine.

Make a button hole in the centre of the top folded edge for the coathanger wire to be pushed through.

If sewing is difficult the pockets can be glued into place, particularly if felt is used.

DAME GONK

You will need:
cone from wool spool
egg boxes, card or plastic
fabric
pink felt
ribbon
glue (e.g. Bostik)

Dame Gonk is made in a similar way to Gonk on page 18.

Cover a cardboard cone with pink felt to make her head and body. Cut two pointed pieces from the egg box and cover these with felt to make arms. Stick them to the body.

To make her dress, wrap a piece of material round the body and arms. Then wrap another piece of material round her waist to make a skirt. Finish off by tying a piece of felt or ribbon round her waist.

Make a hat from pieces of egg box and decorate this with pieces of felt, ribbon and wool.

Using a cone as a basic body shape, you can make lots of different Gonk characters.

PARTY INVITATION

You will need:

medium thick coloured card
coloured tissue paper
paper doily
selection of coloured gummed paper
felt-tip pens
glue (e.g. 'Bostik')

Draw a 6½" (16·5cm) square on the card. Draw a second square ½" (1·3cm) inside the first one, and then divide each side of this square into two. Join these points to form a diamond shape. Using a 2p piece, draw circles round the edge of the card as shown in the diagram and cut away the shaded area. Use this shape to mark out more cards on the coloured card.

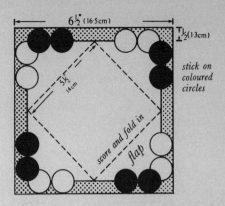

Cut out circles from the gummed paper using the 2p piece again. Stick them over the circles on the card along what will be the outside edge of one side only of each triangle-shaped flap (see patterned circles on the diagram). Stick on more circles to form a bunch of balloons (see picture).

Score and fold the card along the dotted lines forming the diamond (the coloured circles should be on the outside of the card).

Cut two pieces of coloured tissue paper 5½" (14cm) square and glue these to the diamond shape on the inside of the card, leaving the corners free. Fold the corners of the tissue paper to the centre of the card and check that the card closes.

Cut the centre from a small paper doily so that it fits inside the card. Write your invitation on the doily and glue it onto the tissue paper at the centre of the card.

Close the card by folding the flaps without coloured circles, underneath the flaps with coloured circles.

CHRISTMAS STOCKING

You will need:
> *felt or closely-woven material for stocking 20" × 30"*
> *(50cm × 75cm)*
> *small pieces of felt in two or three colours*
> *stranded embroidery cotton*
> *paper for pattern*

Copy the pattern (Fig 1) onto paper making it as large as you have room for on your material. Fold the material in half by bringing together the two shorter sides. Cut out the paper pattern and pin it to the double material. Cut out round the paper pattern allowing 1" (2·5cm) at the top for a hem.

Using the diagrams (Figs 2 and 3) as a guide, make paper patterns for the felt shapes. Use the top of a small cotton reel to draw circles if you wish. Pin these patterns onto felt and cut them out.

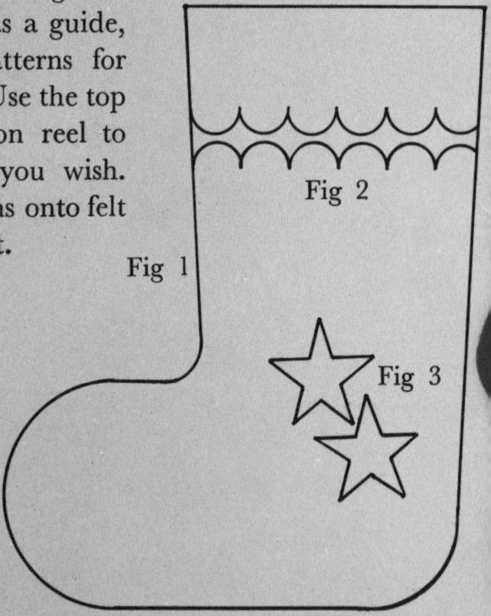

Fig 2

Fig 1

Fig 3

Pin felt shapes to one piece of stocking. Using three strands of embroidery cotton, stitch the shapes into place with blanket stitch. Sew a 1″ (2·5cm) hem along the top edge of both pieces of stocking. Pin the pieces of stocking together with right sides facing and blanket stitch around the edge. Now turn it right side out.

Make a loop from a piece of felt 2″ × 6½″ (5cm × 16cm) folded in half lengthwise, and stitch it in place.

44

TOTEM POLE

You will need:

5 yogurt cartons
a margarine tub
an egg box
black wool
thin card
poster paints
a PVA glue
soap pad (e.g. 'Brillo')

Prepare the cartons by rubbing them down with a soap pad to remove the printing. Paint faces on four of the cartons using poster paints, then glue them together, one on top of the other. Paint the margarine carton and glue it on to form a base. Paint the fifth carton to look like the body of a bird and glue it onto the top of the others.

Cut out two wings from thin card (Fig 1), and paint feathers on both sides of them. Cut two slits, one on each side of the top carton, and slot the wings in position.

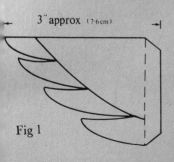

3″ approx (7·6cm)

Fig 1

Make a fluffy pompom, for a head, from black wool (see page 8). Cut the centre section from the base of an egg box to make the eyes and a beak. Paint with poster colours and then glue onto the pompom. Glue the finished head to the top of the totem pole.

PLACE CARDS

You will need:
coloured card of different colours
gold poster paint
coloured paper or felt
glue (e.g. 'Bostik')

Each card is made using the same base. Mark out the base shown in Fig 1 on the coloured card and cut it out. For the flower, owl and cat, this means cutting along the solid line.

To make the angel, cut out the whole shape (Fig 1) and decorate it with poster paints as shown in the picture. Cut out a small circle from gold foil and glue it to the back of the angel's head, to form a halo.

To make the flower, cut out the shapes shown in Fig 2 from coloured felt and glue them together. Stick the finished flower onto the head shape at the top of the base.

To make the cat, either cut out the shapes shown in Fig 3 from coloured paper and glue them onto card, or paint a face onto card and cut it out. Draw on the whiskers and mouth afterwards. Glue the finished cat's head onto the base.

To make the owl cut out the shapes from coloured felt as shown in Fig 4 and glue them together. Finish it off in the same way as the flower.

Write or paint the names on the base of the card underneath the decoration and slot each card together by overlapping tabs **A** and **B**.

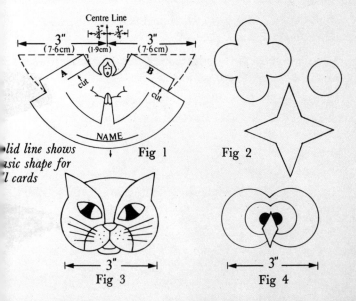

Centre Line

3" (7·6cm)   (1·9cm)   3" (7·6cm)

A   cut   B   cut

NAME

Fig 1

lid line shows
asic shape for
l cards

Fig 2

3"
Fig 3

3"
Fig 4

47

CHRISTMAS TABLE DECORATION

You will need:

½lb (227g) margarine carton
a piece of 'Oasis' to fit inside
    the carton
a doily
crêpe paper
silver paper (cooking foil)

egg boxes
copper wire
poster paint
silver glitter
sewing thread

Cover the outside of the margarine carton with silver paper and place a doily inside. Cover the 'Oasis' with crêpe paper and place it inside the carton.

Cut twelve flower shapes from egg boxes and paint them with white poster paint. Sprinkle the petals with glitter while the paint is still wet.

Cut copper wire into twelve pieces of varying lengths from 5″ to 9″ (12cm to 24cm).

Cut outer petals and small circles for the flower centres, from red crêpe paper.

With small pliers, bend one end of each wire to form a loop. Push the wire through the centres of the small paper circles; then through the centres of the white painted flowers.

Take four or five outer petals and arrange them round the flower. Bind them into place with sewing cotton.

Twist strips of silver paper round the length of copper wire to stop the flower sliding down.

Arrange the flowers in the 'Oasis' with the tallest flowers in the middle.

FABRIC COLLAGE

You will need:
> *a piece of hessian or canvas for background*
> *scraps of material, plain and patterned, lace and felt*
>   *trimmings*
> *glue (e.g. 'Bostik')*
> *thick card for mounting, about 1½" (4cm) smaller all*
>   *round than the background fabric*

A landscape was chosen for this subject because it gives plenty of scope for using different fabrics, textures and trimmings. The cut out shapes can be simple.

Draw shapes to represent hills and fields onto scraps of paper. Cut them out and using them as a paper pattern, cut out the material round the paper.

Lay these pieces onto the background fabric, and arrange them to your satisfaction.

Glue them down with 'Bostik'. Add trees and animals and other details using felt and various trimmings.

Stretch the background material over the card and glue down the edges which fold onto the back. Add a cord to hang up the collage.

GLUING SHEETS OF CARD OR PAPER

Lay sheets of newspaper and change the top sheet each time you have glued something

1 Spread a thin layer of glue onto both surfaces making sure that you go right to the edges. Allow a few minutes for the glue to become tacky

2 Take one of the sheets and line it up along one edge of the sheet you are gluing it to. Smooth the top sheet down evenly with the flat of your hand or a clean cloth

Now change your top sheet of newspaper

GLUING SOLID OBJECTS

Use an impact adhesive such as 'Bostik'

1 Spread glue thinly over the two surfaces to be joined and LEAVE THEM TO DRY

2 Join the two objects together carefully